W.C.FIELDS

I never met a kid I liked.

Edited by
Paul Mason

STANYAN BOOKS

RANDOM HOUSE

For Rock

"I've been drinking professionally
since I was 10...I was a backward
child."

"Fortunately, I'll be dead
when Baby LeRoy's in long pants."

❦

"Your line is 'goo, goo,'
don't muff it."

❦

"I should have gone to night
school, then I'd be able to add."

❦

"Get that kid out of here before
I turn him over my shoulder
and waddle his walloby."

❦

"Any man who hates children can't
be all bad."

"The kid's no trooper,
send him home."

✦

"I'm out of sassperilla, get me
a Shirley Temple."

✦

"Heavens to homossassa.
I've broken the little dolly's
bridgework."

✦

"Don't cry and I'll let you smell
my breath."

✦

"Drat! A rubber dolly, who put
that in here?"

✦

"I never met a kid I liked."

"Hmmm. All dressed up like an open grave."

⁂

"Damnation, the perfume you're wearing is intoxic."

⁂

"We'll spend the weekend hunting chicken livers, yellow breasted chicken livers."

⁂

"My little rocky mountain canary."

⁂

"I'd rather have two girls at 21 each than one girl at 42."

⁂

"You remember the time I knocked Waterfront Nell down?
She'll never forget it."

"When I was young, I'd steal piggy banks from dear little kiddies. Fortunately, when I got older, there were some habits I didn't change."

"Young lady, there is nothing more contemptible than a thief. I should know."

"My dove, my little chickadee,
   my glow worm."

·❦·

"Tell my wife not to wait up for me
   tonight because I won't be home
   for a month."

·❦·

"Ah, my sweet, your eyes are like
   linseed pools."

·❦·

"Don't wait up for me my dear,
   I may play a little parcheesi…"

"Later I'll take you outside and let you ride piggy back on a buzz saw."

"Go sit on a post hole."

"Go out in the traffic and play."

"Take him away before I drive a nail
in his chest."

"Ah, the patter of little feet
around the house. There's nothing
like having a midget for a butler."

"Is this your basketball? It seems to
have fallen under my tire several
times."

"Don't worry, my love, it's only a head cold. I don't plan to be out of work for more than six months."

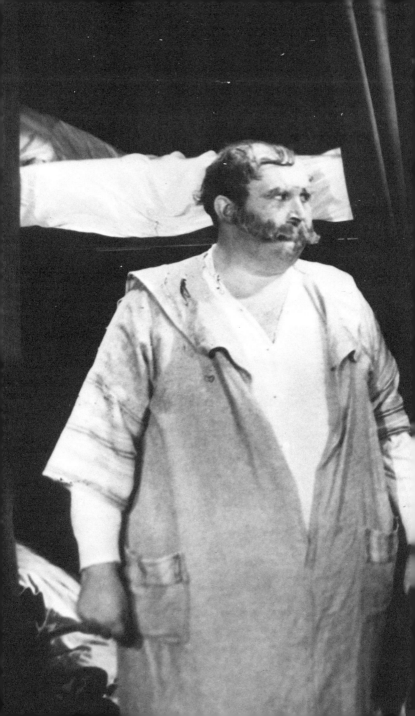

"In the words of my friend
John Barrymore, it was the winter
of my discontent."

❧❦❧

"There may be some things better
than sex, and some things
may be worse, but there is nothing
exactly like it."

❧❦❧

"It ain't a fit night out for man
or beast."

❧❦❧

"Why don't you go back where you
came from if you don't like it here.
Better still, we'll sell you back
Manhattan. Let me see your
baubles."

❧❦❧

"We're going to the Arctic. We've
been on an expedition to hunt the
Mexican Hairless…for scientific
purposes, of course…see you
around 1906 if we come through."

"You can't hurt a child dropping him
on his head, at that age
their heads are soft anyway."

※

"Get away from me you little
bastard! For two cents—or even
one—I'd kick in your teeth."

※

"Show me a kid with ringlets and
I'll show you a purple rose."

※

"How do you suppose your bicycle
got in my basement?"

"The kid's in there drinking my best gin. Get him out of here before I drive a spike through his head and make him a decanter."

✦❖✦

"I never smoked a cigarette until I was 9."

✦❖✦

"If the 4th of July was good enough for George Washington, it should be good enough for you. Now go out in the parade and play. Try beating off your drum."

✦❖✦

"The bastard offered me 50 per cent interest. It was a shabby way to treat a boy in his teens."

"Your kid looks like a monkey."

"I've been thinking about the little newsies out there peddling their papers in the cold. Some of them the sole support of their mothers…I thought I might do something for them this Christmas; on second thought…"

"She suffered a great deal, her mother was an acrobat."

"I'm not given to rash statements, but either he goes or I go with him."

"He'd make a great butter churn, just the right size."

"You'll have to forgive her, her washing machine's clogged."

"J. Whipsnade's the name, of the Philadelphia Whipsnades."

"Where did you get it? Take it back."

"She was built like a brick chickenhouse."

"I played backgammon all my life. Stand back and watch my dust."

◦※◦

"Lemonade and mind it's not too tart."

◦※◦

"Later we'll drive home in a single saddle surrey."

◦※◦

"I'll make her a lady if I have to knock her down to do it."

"Here kid, catch!"

"Set up the weegie board…the one with the real weegies."

⋅⋅⋅※∭※⋅⋅⋅

"I want to look as spiffy as a penguin, on second thought a penguin in sports clothes."

⋅⋅⋅※∭※⋅⋅⋅

"Lay out my semi-precious watch chain."

⋅⋅⋅※∭※⋅⋅⋅

"By the time I was 15, I could play the Bugle Call Rag on a comb."

"Will it hold water?"

"They're just not making gravy boats like they used to."

"Jumping spotted swordfish."

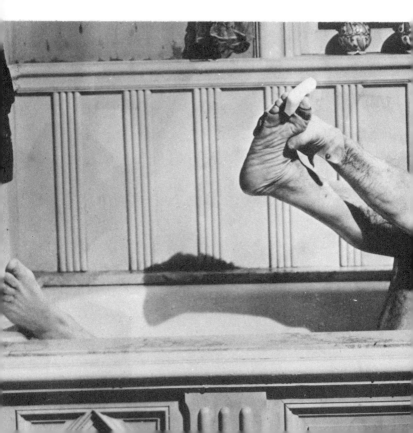

"Naturally I'll do my pool act
in this picture, it would be
ridiculous not to."

"All landlords should get the
electric chair. For those with
children, you might increase the
voltage."

"Great Caesar's ghost!"

"Stand up and fight like a man."

"She was wearing a wig, but there
   was no accounting for her teeth."

⚜

"Either you're drunk or your
   braces are lopsided."

⚜

"Stay in this room and don't
   fall out the window unless it's
   absolutely necessary."

⚜

"Cross my heart and hope to eat
   my weight in goslings."

"I need a dollar to pay for my room."

"He looks just like his father, but I wouldn't like him if he didn't."

"Great stars! It's the chamber pot that's been missing from my chamber."

"Is he one of a kind or part of a matched set?"

"He was stuttering. I think he had the German measles."

"Later the good fairy will put a dime under your pillow."

"Get the kid a limousine, he'll never make it with the load he's carrying."

"The mustache stays, what's wrong with it?"

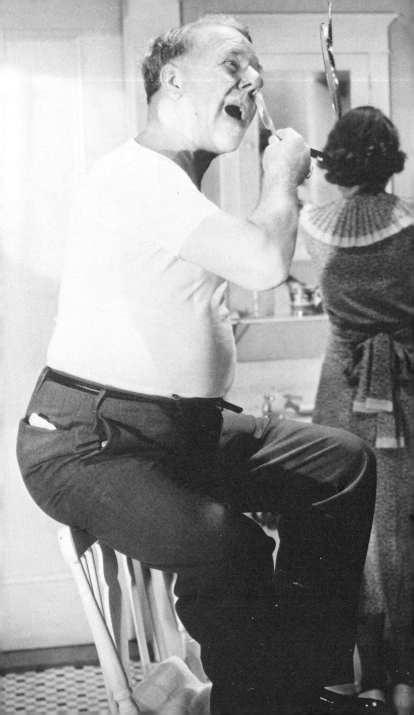

"My heart is a bargain today,
  will you take it?"

⁓⊰❈⊱⁓

Pardon me while I repair for
  repairs."

⁓⊰❈⊱⁓

"Now that I'm here I'll dally
  in the valley, and believe me
  I can dally."

⁓⊰❈⊱⁓

"Ah, your lips are like tiny
  little wine presses."

⁓⊰❈⊱⁓

"Mind you, I'm on your side,
  but the cook's been carrying
  tales about you and the upstairs
  maid."

⁓⊰❈⊱⁓

"Balderdash!"

⁓⊰❈⊱⁓

"He had a nasty fall. I think
  it scrambled his adenoids."

"You want to make something of it?"

"On the whole, I'd rather have been in Philadelphia."